Twenty–One Days to Baghdad

A Chronicle of the Iraq War

Twenty–One Days to Baghdad

A Chronicle of the Iraq War

REUTERS

Published by **Prentice Hall**

Library of Congress Cataloging-in-Publication Data

A CIP catalog record for this book can be obtained from the Library of Congress

Publisher: Tim Moore
Executive editor: Jim Boyd
Director of production: Sophie Papanikolaou
Production supervisor: Nicholas Radhuber
Marketing manager: John Pierce
Manufacturing manager: Alexis Heydt-Long

Editorial assistant: Linda Ramagnano
Cover design director: Jerry Votta
Cover designer: Anthony Gemmellaro
Art director: Gail Cocker-Bogusz
Interior design and page layout: Meg Van Arsdale

Reuters:
Executive editor: Stephen Jukes
Coordinating editor: Peter Millership
Commercial manager: Alisa Bowen
Front cover art photographer: Goran Tomasevic

In compiling this book, thanks go to many people. At Reuters, Lance Bell, Steve Crisp, David Cutler, Giles Elgood, Jason Pickersgill, Mair Salts, Alexia Singh, David Viggers.

This book would not have been possible without the brave and committed multimedia team of Reuters journalists who covered the Iraq War and the editors and production desks supporting them.

© 2003 Reuters
Published by Pearson Education, Inc.
Publishing as Reuters Prentice Hall
Upper Saddle River, NJ 07458

Prentice Hall offers excellent discounts on this book when ordered in quantity for bulk purchases or special sales. For more information, please contact:
U.S. Corporate and Government Sales
1-800-382-3419
corpsales@pearsontechgroup.com

For sales outside of the U.S., please contact:
International Sales
1-317-581-3793
international@pearsontechgroup.com

Printed in the United States of America

1st printing

ISBN 0-13-143165-X

Pearson Education Ltd.
Pearson Education Australia PTY, Limited
Pearson Education Singapore, Pte. Ltd.
Pearson Education North Asia Ltd.
Pearson Education Canada, Ltd.
Pearson Educación de Mexico, S.A. de C.V.
Pearson Education—Japan
Pearson Education Malaysia, Pte. Ltd.

Contents

Narrative by Giles Elgood

Taras Protsyuk

This book is dedicated to Reuters cameraman
Taras Protsyuk,
killed in Baghdad by a U.S. tank shell on April 8,
and his colleagues who were injured in the blast—
Faleh Kheiber, Samia Nakhoul and Paul Pasquale.
We also remember Spanish cameraman
José Couso,
killed in the same incident at the Palestine Hotel,
and all other journalists who lost their lives covering the war in Iraq.

Twenty–One Days to Baghdad

A Chronicle of the Iraq War

Striking at Saddam

Buildup and Day 1

March 20

For weeks the Pentagon had let it be known that Iraqis could expect the war to start with a colossal bombardment of Baghdad. It was to be an aerial assault that would, in the jargon of the U.S. military, "shock and awe" Saddam Hussein and persuade his forces that defeat was inevitable.

In fact the Iraq War did not begin like that. Seizing the opportunity provided by a timely intelligence tip, the U.S. field commander, Gen. Tommy Franks, unleashed a targeted dawn wave of cruise missiles and warplanes at a Baghdad bunker where Saddam and other members of the Iraqi leadership were believed to have gathered.

Fireballs lit up the night sky over Baghdad, and, as dawn broke, the capital's stunned residents could see huge black clouds billowing over the skyline.

The goal was to "decapitate" the Iraqi top ranks and perhaps bring the war to a swifter conclusion than anyone on the U.S. side had dared to hope. There were suggestions that Saddam had been killed or wounded

when the bunker-busting bombs hit home. That was apparently not to be. Saddam appeared on television, grim faced and bespectacled, to denounce U.S. President George W. Bush as a criminal. The Bush administration expressed doubts about when the videotape had been made.

With Saddam's fate unclear at that stage and no signs of an Iraqi surrender, the war began in earnest, with more raids on Baghdad and a military push across the border from Kuwait by U.S. and British ground troops. Australian special forces had also moved into Iraq.

It was a process that had been set in motion months before. Bush had publicly shifted the focus of American attention from al Qaeda to Iraq, naming Iraq alongside Iran and North Korea as members of an "axis of evil" after the September 11 attacks.

A U.N. resolution calling on Saddam to disarm had been secured in November 2002 and later that month U.N.

arms inspectors were sent into Iraq to search for biological, chemical and nuclear weapons.

As the fault lines in the U.N. Security Council became more clearly defined—France, Germany and Russia threw their weight solidly against the war—Washington dropped plans for a second resolution authorizing war and accelerated its military buildup in the Gulf.

With British participation, a strike force that totaled 270,000 service men and women assembled on aircraft carriers and warships, and at land bases in Kuwait and elsewhere in the Gulf region. The size of the force was less than half that of the Gulf War in 1991, and the number of nations contributing significant forces was much less.

However, the U.S.-led force was armed with weaponry of a destructive power and precision never seen before, and against it stood an Iraqi military that had been defeated 12 years earlier and that had been weakened by years of sanctions.

President Bush and British Prime Minister Tony Blair, along with their other main European ally, Spanish Prime Minister José Maria Aznar, held a council of war on the Azores islands in the mid-Atlantic as the clock ticked down to conflict. Millions turned out at anti-war demonstrations in major cities around the world, with little discernible effect on the march to war.

Then, on March 17, President Bush spoke to the American people. Iraq, he said from the White House, would not disarm as long as Saddam remained in power. Therefore, Saddam and his two sons, Uday and Qusay, had 48 hours to leave the country.

"Their refusal to do so will result in military conflict commenced at the time of our choosing," the president declared.

Sirens sounded in Baghdad about 90 minutes after the U.S. deadline expired. The first air strike had been unleashed.

A CH-46 helicopter painted with th
U.S. flag on a refueling and supp
operation in the Gulf, March 15, 200

REUTERS/John Schults

Flight deck crews are engulfed in steam as they signal to the pilot of an F/A-18 Hornet fighter preparing for takeoff from the USS Kitty Hawk in the northern Gulf, March 14, 2003.

REUTERS/Paul Hanna

OPPOSING GROUND FORCES IN THE IRAQ CONFLICT

The United States and Britain assembled up to 270,000 troops to oppose Iraq's army of about 300,000 regular troops plus almost 100,000 Republican Guard troops

Although numerically superior, Iraq's army relied on out-of-date technology and half of all equipment lacked spare parts

U.S. / BRITAIN

Main battle tanks: 750

The principal U.S. tank used in the 1991 Gulf War, the **M1 Abrams** outranged Iraqi tanks by an average of 1,000 yards

M1

Type	Speed	Weight	Crew	Main armament
M1	45mph	60 tons	4	105mm gun
M1A2	42mph	70 tons	4	120mm gun
Challenger 2 🇬🇧	35mph	63 tons	4	120mm gun

Reconnaissance / AIFVs: 600

Highly effective during the Gulf War, the **M2 / M3 Bradley** destroyed more Iraqi armored vehicles than the M1 Abrams

M2

Type	Speed	Weight	Crew	Main armament
Scimitar 🇬🇧	50mph	8 tons	3	30mm gun
M2	45mph	23 tons	3+6	25mm gun
M3	45mph	23 tons	3+2	25mm gun
Warrior 🇬🇧	45mph	24 tons	3+7	30mm gun

APCs: 600

The **M113** carries up to 11 troops and is operated by the armed forces of more than 50 countries, including Iraq

M113

Type	Speed	Weight	Crew	Main armament
M113	41mph	14 tons	2+11	12.7mm MG
Spartan 🇬🇧	50mph	8 tons	2+5	7.62mm MG

Artillery: 150+

M109

The 155mm **M109 Paladin** self-propelled howitzer equipping U.S. infantry brigades has a range of 19 miles

Type	Caliber	Total
Towed	105mm and 155mm	–
Self-propelled	155mm	150
Multiple rocket launchers	227mm	–

IRAQ

Main battle tanks: 2,200

All 700 of Iraq's remaining force of relatively-modern **T-72s** were allocated to elite Republican Guard divisions

T-72

Type	Speed	Weight	Crew	Main armament
T-72	37mph	45 tons	3	125mm gun
T-62	31mph	42 tons	4	115mm gun
T-54 / T-55	31mph	41 tons	4	100mm gun

Reconnaissance / AIFVs: 1,400

Iraq had 900 of the relatively modern **BMP-1** and **BMP-2 armored** vehicle, equipped with anti-tank missiles

BMP-1

Type	Speed	Weight	Crew	Main armament
BRDM-2	59mph	7 tons	4	14.5mm MG
AML-90	56mph	6 tons	3	90mm gun
BMP-1	40mph	14 tons	3+8	73mm gun
BMP-2	40mph	14 tons	3+7	30mm gun

APCs: 2,400

Exported to more than 40 countries worldwide, Iraq had large numbers of the Russian-made **BTR-60** wheeled troop carrier

BTR-60

Type	Speed	Weight	Crew	Main armament
BTR-50	28mph	14 tons	2+20	7.62mm MG
BTR-60	50mph	10 tons	2+12	12.7mm MG

Artillery: 2,250

Among Iraq's mix of mainly Russian and U.S.-made artillery was the 122mm **2S1** self-propelled howitzer with a range of nine miles

2S1

Type	Caliber	Total
Towed	105mm to 155mm	1,900
Self-propelled	122mm to 155mm	150
Multiple rocket launchers	107mm to 262mm	200

AIFV = armored infantry fighting vehicle   MG = machinegun   🇬🇧 = British forces
APC = armored personnel carrier   Illustrations not to scale. All equipment numbers are estimates
Sources: GlobalSecurity.org, Federation of American Scientists, Center for Defense Information, British Army

REUTERS

British troops gather for a briefing by U.S. Lt. Gen. Jeff Conway, Commanding General 1st Marine Expeditionary Force, in the Kuwaiti desert, March 14, 2003.

REUTERS/Ministry of Defence/Paul Jarvis

British soldiers from 29 Commando Regiment Royal Artillery listen to a sermon from the regimental chaplain during a field service in the Kuwaiti desert, March 16, 2003.

REUTERS/Stephen Hird

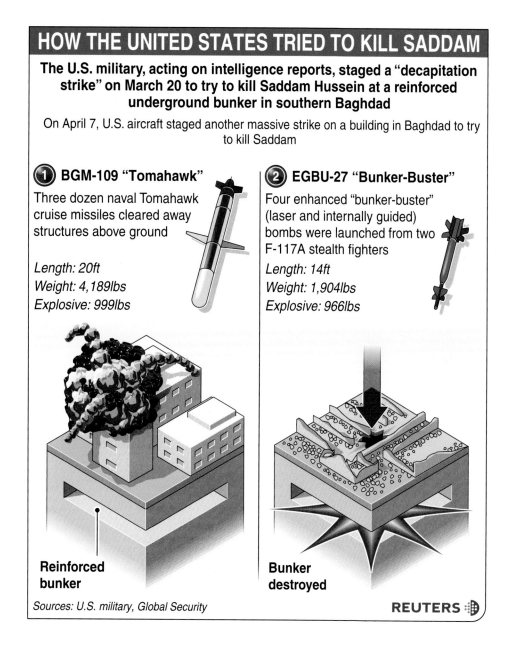

HOW THE UNITED STATES TRIED TO KILL SADDAM

The U.S. military, acting on intelligence reports, staged a "decapitation strike" on March 20 to try to kill Saddam Hussein at a reinforced underground bunker in southern Baghdad

On April 7, U.S. aircraft staged another massive strike on a building in Baghdad to try to kill Saddam

① BGM-109 "Tomahawk"

Three dozen naval Tomahawk cruise missiles cleared away structures above ground

Length: 20ft
Weight: 4,189lbs
Explosive: 999lbs

② EGBU-27 "Bunker-Buster"

Four enhanced "bunker-buster" (laser and internally guided) bombs were launched from two F-117A stealth fighters

Length: 14ft
Weight: 1,904lbs
Explosive: 966lbs

Reinforced bunker

Bunker destroyed

Sources: U.S. military, Global Security

REUTERS

British soldiers from 29 Commando Regiment Royal Artillery fire their 105 mm light guns from a position in the Kuwaiti desert at targets in southern Iraq during the first night of the campaign, March 20, 2003.

REUTERS/Stephen Hird

Saddam Hussein appears on state television three hours after the United States launched a war to overthrow him, March 20, 2003. It was impossible to be certain the broadcast was live. The conflict started with what the U.S. military said was a "decapitation strike" to try and kill Saddam.

REUTERS/Reuters Television

The Iron Fist

Days 2–5

March 21–24

Rolling across the desert, U.S. armored columns began the invasion of Iraq, setting in motion the land war. Gen. Tommy Franks promised "a campaign characterized by shock, by surprise, by flexibility, by the employment of precise munitions on a scale never before seen and by the application of overwhelming force." In short, Franks said the campaign he had planned was "unlike any other in history."

Another wave of cruise missiles hit Baghdad, targeting the strongholds of Saddam Hussein's special Republican Guard, a presidential palace and offices of senior leadership figures. Wave after wave of warplanes struck the Iraqi capital, setting buildings ablaze and sending plumes of smoke high into the hazy sky. President Bush's Operation Iraqi Freedom was now fully underway.

To the south, British and U.S. troops seized oil installations and moved in on the Iraqi port of Umm Qasr. A U.S. Marine raised the Stars and Stripes over the port, but it was quickly removed to avoid inflaming local sensitivities.

A handful of oil wells were set ablaze by the Iraqis, but quick seizure of the important Rumaila field averted an ecological catastrophe of the sort seen in 1991 when retreating Iraqi forces torched the Kuwaiti oil fields.

U.S. Defense Secretary Donald Rumsfeld said Saddam was now "history" as his grip on the country weakened. In southern Iraq, the commander of Iraq's 51st Division, which numbered several thousand troops, surrendered to U.S. Marines.

As waves of armored vehicles pushed into Iraqi territory, viewers could watch the war up close on live television, thanks to satellite technology and correspondents "embedded" with military units.

The allies suffered their first casualties of the war when eight British soldiers and four U.S. airmen died in a helicopter crash on the Iraqi border. A U.S. serviceman who killed two U.S. soldiers and wounded 14 others in

a grenade attack at a tented command center in Kuwait caused more dismay.

Americans were also shocked when Iraqi television showed film of four dead U.S. soldiers and broadcast interviews with five U.S. prisoners of war taken near the southern city of Nassiriya. An angry Rumsfeld said that the videotape violated the Geneva Convention on the treatment of prisoners of war.

U.S. armored units were speeding north toward Baghdad and British tanks approached Basra, Iraq's second largest city, but the allies did not have it all their own way. On the war's fourth day, Iraqi troops and paramilitary fighters managed to hold up the U.S. advance, inflicting casualties and taking prisoners. A guerrilla counterattack by Saddam's Fedayeen—a guerrilla group little heard of before the start of the war—stopped a major thrust to the north by U.S. Marines, who took casualties in fighting as they sought to cross the

Euphrates at Nassiriya. There was also more fighting at Najaf, further to the north.

Iraqi resistance was somewhat stiffer than expected, and tactics seemed designed to harass the U.S. forces as they advanced hundreds of miles through enemy territory. In the southern cities of Umm Qasr and Basra, fighting continued for longer than had been anticipated.

"The enemy we're fighting," said Lt. Gen. William Wallace, the senior U.S. Army officer in Kuwait, "is a bit different from the one we'd war-gamed against." Nor did Iraqis in the south of the country immediately welcome the U.S. and British troops as liberators, as Washington had hoped.

That perhaps was hardly surprising. The southern Shi'ites had felt badly betrayed after the first Gulf War, when they rose up against Saddam and, left to fend for themselves without U.S. help, were ruthlessly crushed by Baghdad. They also were not yet confident that Saddam's police state was a thing of the past.

A U.S. B-52 bomber takes off from a British Royal Air Force base in Fairford, Gloucestershire, western England, March 21, 2003.

REUTERS/Darren Staples

A British armored convoy rolls into
southern Iraq, March 22, 2003.

REUTERS/Oleg Popov

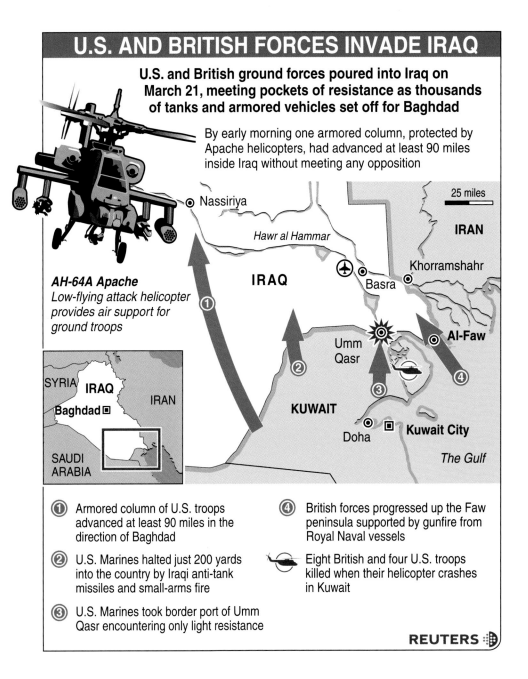

U.S. AND BRITISH FORCES INVADE IRAQ

U.S. and British ground forces poured into Iraq on March 21, meeting pockets of resistance as thousands of tanks and armored vehicles set off for Baghdad

By early morning one armored column, protected by Apache helicopters, had advanced at least 90 miles inside Iraq without meeting any opposition

AH-64A Apache
Low-flying attack helicopter provides air support for ground troops

25 miles

Nassiriya

Hawr al Hammar

IRAN

IRAQ

Khorramshahr

Basra

Al-Faw

① ②

Umm Qasr

③

④

KUWAIT

Doha

Kuwait City

The Gulf

SYRIA
IRAQ
Baghdad
IRAN
SAUDI ARABIA

① Armored column of U.S. troops advanced at least 90 miles in the direction of Baghdad

② U.S. Marines halted just 200 yards into the country by Iraqi anti-tank missiles and small-arms fire

③ U.S. Marines took border port of Umm Qasr encountering only light resistance

④ British forces progressed up the Faw peninsula supported by gunfire from Royal Naval vessels

Eight British and four U.S. troops killed when their helicopter crashes in Kuwait

REUTERS

Marines take cover from Iraqi fire during the early stage of the push into southern Iraq to take control of the main port of Umm Qasr, March 21, 2003.

REUTERS/Desmond Boylan

An explosion rocks one of Saddam Hussein's palaces in Baghdad during massive air strikes, March 21, 2003. Military analysts had warned Iraq to brace for U.S. "shock and awe" tactics.

REUTERS/Goran Tomasevic

Baghdad ablaze during air strikes,
March 21, 2003.

REUTERS/Goran Tomasevic

Iraqi civilians caught in the crossfire as Marines push into southern Iraq to take control of the main port of Umm Qasr, March 21, 2003.

REUTERS/Desmond Boylan

Polish special forces hold a captured
Iraqi man on a U.S. Navy Seals boat in
Umm Qasr, March 23, 2003.

REUTERS/Desmond Boylan

In this sequence, a Marine lowers the Iraqi flag at the entrance to the port of Umm Qasr, replacing it with the Stars and Stripes and the Marine Corps flag, March 21, 2003. Some time later, Marines returned and removed the flags. No official reason was given, but the U.S. military had stressed that it wished to be seen as a force of liberation, not occupation.

REUTERS/Desmond Boylan

A U.S. F-117A Nighthawk stealth warplane at a base in Kuwait after a mission over Iraq, March 22, 2003.

REUTERS/Russell Boyce

Marines ride in a truck during an early
stage of the push into southern Iraq
to take control of Umm Qasr, March
21, 2003.

REUTERS/Desmond Boylan

British Royal Marines escort captured
Iraqis in Umm Qasr, March 22, 2003.

REUTERS/Desmond Boylan

The body of an Iraqi soldier lies wrapped in a blanket close to his trench position following a lightning assault by British commandos on the Faw peninsula in southern Iraq, March 22, 2003.

REUTERS/Stephen Hird

Iraqi soldiers lie on the ground after they surrender to Marines in the desert in southern Iraq, March 22, 2003.

REUTERS/Damir Sagolj

A U.S. soldier guards a group of Iraqi prisoners of war as a British Warrior armored fighting vehicle passes in the Iraqi town of Safwan, near the Kuwaiti border, March 22, 2003.

REUTERS/Chris Helgren

Marines under fire in Umm Qasr, March 23, 2003. Two days later, U.S. and British forces declared the port "safe and open."

REUTERS/Desmond Boylan

A boy tosses a cigarette to Iraqi prisoners of war by a road leading to the southern city of Basra, March 23, 2003.

REUTERS/Jerry Lampen

Sandstorm

Days 6–15

March 25–April 3

After a lightning thrust north to within 60 miles of Baghdad, the U.S. advance appeared to pause. A mighty sandstorm swept through Iraq, cutting visibility to less than five yards in some places, and, as the dust swirled, there was growing criticism of the U.S. military plan.

Supply lines more than 200 miles long were too extended and were vulnerable to hit-and-run attacks, said the armchair generals and other critical analysts in Washington, and the U.S.-led force was too small to have attempted such an ambitious advance. In an apparent acknowledgement that the fighting was tougher than expected, the Pentagon said another 100,000 troops were being ordered into Iraq.

U.S. officers in the field spoke of a temporary halt in the advance of between four and six days to allow their tired and sand-coated soldiers to resupply after their epic dash through the desert, but commanders in the rear insisted the war was being pressed home on several fronts.

Southern Iraq faced a growing humanitarian crisis, with inhabitants suffering from shortages of water. In Baghdad, at least 62 people were killed in an air raid on a market in a busy district of the city. The United States promised to investigate whether its forces were to blame.

On the battlefield, U.S. soldiers faced attacks from Iraqis dressed in civilian clothes and who fired when waving the white flag of surrender. At a checkpoint near the Shi'ite holy city of Najaf, four U.S. soldiers died when a car bomb exploded.

Iraq vowed to step up such suicide attacks and said that thousands of Arabs had come to Baghdad to "martyr" themselves in order to defeat the U.S.-led invasion. In a separate incident near Najaf, U.S. troops discovered that they had killed seven women and children when they opened fire on a vehicle that failed to obey orders to stop. As well as this a number of allied soldiers were killed in what the U.S. military refers to as "friendly fire"—when forces accidentally kill members of their own side.

Iraqis celebrated what they saw as setbacks for the U.S.-led forces by dancing on a downed Apache Longbow helicopter near the city of Kerbala, 70 miles southwest of Baghdad.

"We've never said it was going to be quick," said Air Force Gen. Richard Myers, chairman of the Joint Chiefs of Staff. "We've never said it was going to be easy."

If the advance on Baghdad appeared to lose momentum for a while, there was uplifting news for the United States in the rescue of Pfc. Jessica Lynch, a 19-year-old from Palestine, West Virginia, whose maintenance convoy was ambushed by Iraqi forces after it took a wrong turn. Grainy nightvision video showed U.S. special forces saving Private Lynch in a daring helicopter raid on the hospital where she had been held for 10 days with injuries that included two broken legs and a broken arm.

Several days earlier, U.S. airborne forces parachuted into Kurdish-held territory, securing an airfield that would serve as the bridgehead for an important northern front against Saddam. Now, after delays, apparent setbacks and mounting criticism at home, this operation gave a clear sign that U.S. forces were in a position to tighten the noose around the main prize—Saddam Hussein's Baghdad.

An Iraqi man waves his AK-47 rifle in front of a U.S. Apache helicopter in the Hindiya district, 70 miles southwest of Baghdad, March 24, 2003. At the time Iraqi officials claimed it was brought down by a shot fired by a farmer, something the United States denied.

REUTERS/Faleh Kheiber

Iraqis celebrate on a U.S. Apache helicopter in the Hindiya district, March 24, 2003. On the same day, Britain confirmed its first soldier lost in combat.

REUTERS/Faleh Kheiber

An Army soldier stand[...] guard by a burning oil well [...] Iraq's vast southern Ruma[...] oil fields, March 30, 2003.

REUTERS/Yannis Behrakis

An injured U.S. serviceman is carried by stretcher off a military aircraft at Ramstein U.S. Air Force Base in southwest Germany, March 29, 2003.

REUTERS/Dylan Martinez

Six-year-old Tyler Jordan watches as the casket of his father, Marine Gunnery Sgt. Philip Jordan, is carried from Holy Family Church after his funeral in Enfield, Connecticut, April 2, 2003. Sgt. Jordan was killed during fighting outside Nassiriya on March 23.

REUTERS/Jim Bourg

A Marine points his rifle at a group of
Iraqis stopped on a road in central
Iraq near Qal'at Sukkar, March 27,
2003.

REUTERS/Damir Sagolj

A doctor with the Marines cradles an Iraqi girl in central Iraq, March 29, 2003.

REUTERS/Damir Sagolj

A Marine carries a shocked Iraqi girl
caught in the crossfire in central Iraq,
March 29, 2003.

REUTERS/Damir Sagolj

An Army soldier cleans his face after driving in a sandstorm south of the city of Kerbala, March 25, 2003. The storm blew in over U.S. troops advancing on Baghdad, cutting visibility and hampering operations.

REUTERS/Peter Andrews

An Army combat engineer enjoys a cigarette as he relaxes between the cities of Najaf and Kerbala, and a sandstorm turns the daylight orange, March 26, 2003. The sandstorm slowed the epic armored dash to Baghdad and brought fears that U.S. supply lines were vulnerable.

REUTERS/Kai Pfaffenbach

A SANDSTORM HITS THE U.S. ARMORED COLUMN

■ Effects of a sandstorm on advancing U.S. troops

Cruise missiles
As the final approach to target necessitates ground study, they may be less accurate

Fighters and bombers
Not affected

Support vehicles
Can suffer mechanical failure. Drivers can't see obstacles along the road, slowing down the column as they can get lost or ambushed

Helicopters
Most sensitive to bad weather conditions. Risk mechanical failure or can be destabilized by winds

Armored vehicles
Not affected, navigation system equipment allows them to progress through storm

Soldiers
Infantry soldiers' action is impaired. Poor visibility gives the column's attackers an advantage

Armored columns
Heavy equipment trailers and armored vehicles travel at different speeds through a storm forcing the column to stretch. The rear part of the convoy then becomes more vulnerable to attack

Even if infrared navigation systems are not affected by a sandstorm, visual reconnaissance of targets is harder (risk of friendly fire incidents)

Source: Military Advisor

REUTERS

U.S. Army Gen. Tommy Franks gestures as he tells a news conference that his military campaign to topple Saddam Hussein and his ruling elite is on track, As Sayliya Camp, outside Doha, Qatar, March 30, 2003. "We're in fact on plan. And where we stand today is not only acceptable in my view, it is truly remarkable," he said. "There have been some pundits who have indicated we may be in an operational pause," Franks said. "It's simply not the case."

REUTERS/Tim Aubry

An Iraqi man is stopped for questioning outside Basra, March 30, 2003.

REUTERS/Jerry Lampen

An Iraqi boy and a small child ride a camel near U.S. tanks in a sandstorm in the desert, south of the city of Kerbala, March 26, 2003.

REUTERS/Peter Andrews

An armed Iraqi passes a burning car after an air strike in Baghdad, March 26, 2003.

REUTERS/Goran Tomasevic

A man covers the body of an Iraqi killed in an explosion in a busy residential area of Baghdad, March 26, 2003. U.S. defense officials said an errant U.S. missile may have caused the deadly blast, but that anti-aircraft artillery or missiles fired by Iraqis may also have been responsible.

REUTERS/Goran Tomasevic

An Iraqi girl holds her sister as she waits for her mother to bring food bought in Basra, March 29, 2003.

REUTERS/Jerry Lampen

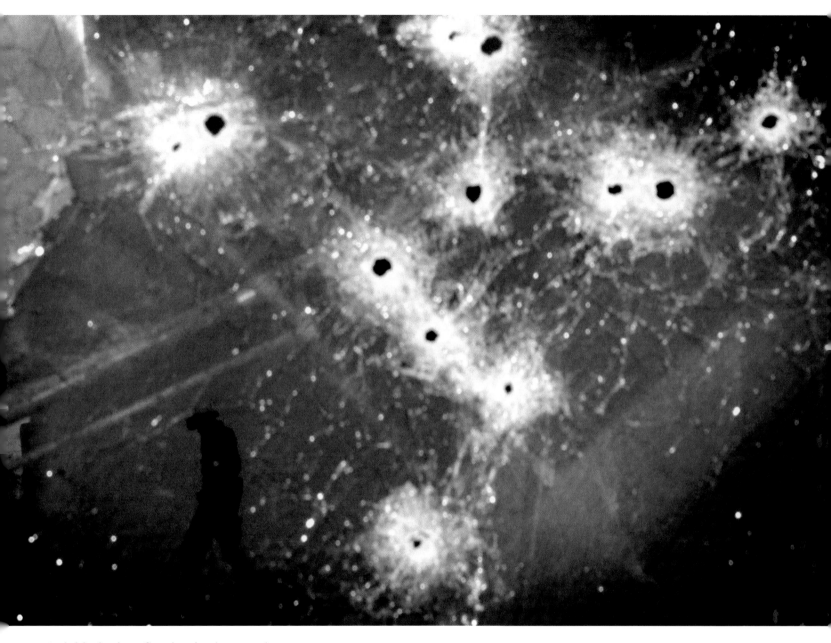

A Marine's reflection in the wreckage of a bus full of dead Iraqi men, which was attacked earlier on a road in central Iraq near Qal 'at Sukkar, March 27, 2003. Reporters counted four corpses outside the bus, and Marines said another 16 were inside. All the bodies were adult men, wearing a mixture of civilian and military clothing and had papers that appeared to identify them as Iraqi Republican Guard.

REUTERS/Damir Sagolj

Marines lead away captured Iraqi soldiers after a firefight in central Iraq, March 29, 2003.

REUTERS/Damir Sagolj

British commandos fire 105mm guns
during a night attack in southern Iraq,
March 26, 2003.

REUTERS/Stephen Hird

A family caught up in the fighti
flees past a destroyed Iraqi T-55 ta
after a mortar bomb attack on Brit
Army positions in Basra, March 2
2003.

REUTERS/Chris Helgren

An Iraqi man is taken away for questioning by a British soldier outside Basra, March 30, 2003.

REUTERS/Jerry Lampen

A child sitting on his father's shoulders fights for a box of food as people grab at packages handed out by British forces from the back of a truck in the southern town of Safwan, March 31, 2003.

REUTERS/Russell Boyce

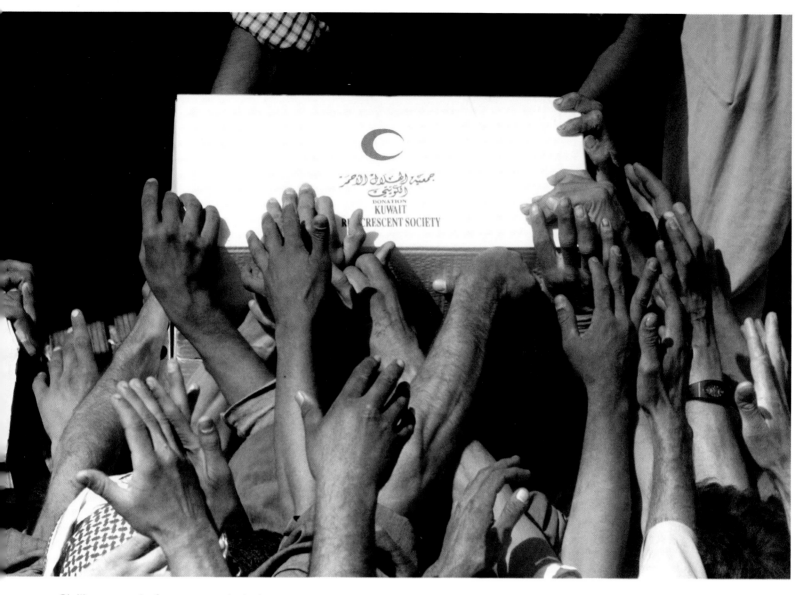

Civilians reach for a parcel during a
Red Crescent aid distribution in
Safwan, March 28, 2003.

REUTERS/Yannis Behrakis

Marines backed up by helicopters secure a key bridge over the Tigris River, April 2, 2003. Two days later the Marines would take Baghdad airport as a prelude to storming into the heart of the Iraqi capital.

REUTERS/Oleg Popov

Iraqi prisoners of war sit behind razor
wire by the side of the road to
Baghdad, April 3, 2003.

REUTERS/Kai Pfaffenbach

A British Army Warrior vehicle passes a destroyed Iraqi T-55 tank, south of Basra, April 2, 2003.

REUTERS/Chris Helgren

Marines at a bridge over the Tigris River, April 2, 2003. American armor was on the move and was preparing for the final push to Baghdad.

REUTERS/Oleg Popov

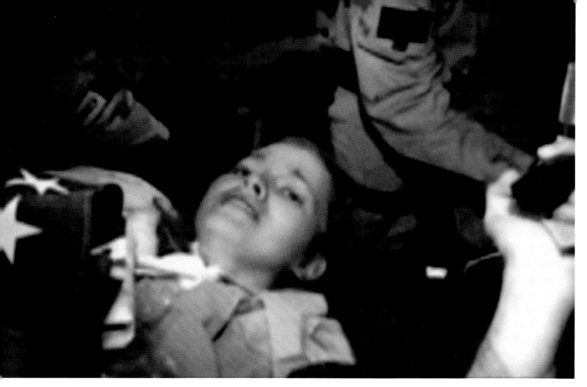

Saving Private Lynch. Undated combat camera video shows 19-year-old Pfc. Jessica Lynch being rescued by U.S. special forces from a hospital in Nassiriya, southern Iraq, where she was being held. "Jessica Lynch, we are United States soldiers and we're here to protect you and take you home," one of the commandos said, in a scene which could have been scripted by Hollywood. Dazed and frightened, it took her a while to understand. "I'm an American soldier, too," she replied. The raiders whisked her on a stretcher to a waiting helicopter. Holding the hand of an Army Ranger doctor Lynch said, "Please don't let anybody leave me." Video of the drama was shown as part of a media briefing at Camp As Sayliya, Qatar, April 2, 2003.

REUTERS/Handout/U.S. Central Command

An undated family photograph of Lynch made available to Reuters.

REUTERS/Handout

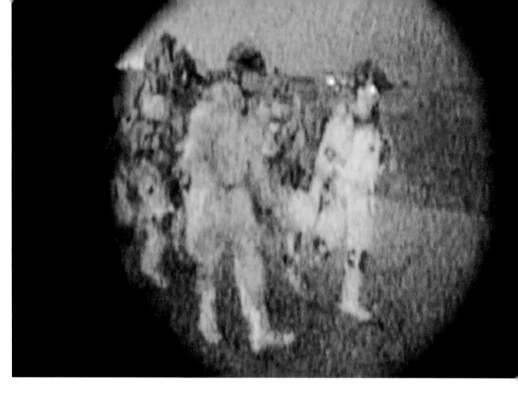

Lynch, from Palestine, West Virginia, filmed with a night vision lens being stretchered from a helicopter after her rescue. She was held captive for 10 days. The image was released to the media, April 2, 2003.

REUTERS/U.S. Defense Department video

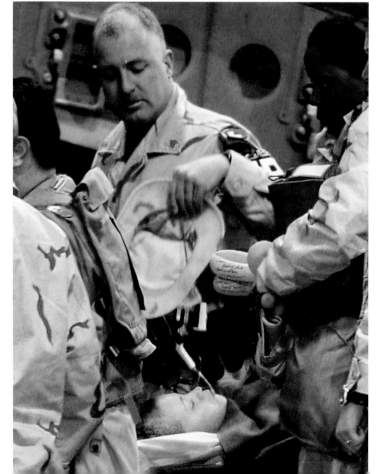

Lynch arrives at Ramstein U.S. Air Force base in southwest Germany to recover from her ordeal, April 3, 2003.

REUTERS/Vincent Kessler

Dagger at the Heart

Days 16–20

April 4–8

U.S. armored units began their final push toward Baghdad, and Saddam Hussein issued a rallying call, urging Iraqis to wage a holy war against the invaders.

Threatening "nonconventional" action, the battered Iraqi leadership appeared to be preparing not to deploy chemical or biological weapons, but to make mass use of human shields, suicide attacks and last-ditch street-by-street fighting—a scenario that U.S. military officials feared could turn the taking of the Iraqi capital into a "big battle."

Once again, it did not quite turn out that way. U.S. forces moved into Saddam International Airport on the outskirts of the city and renamed the facility Baghdad International. The Americans had achieved a strategic goal that also sent a strong political message to Iraqi leaders. Two days later, the first U.S. aircraft, a C-130 military transporter, touched down at the airport, where 7,000 U.S. troops had taken up positions.

Iraqi television showed footage of what it said was Saddam being cheered on the streets of Baghdad, and his information minister, Mohammed Saeed al-Sahaf, said Iraqis were ready to carry out suicide attacks on the Americans. In a series of increasingly surreal briefings and statements, al-Sahaf declared that U.S. forces were "committing suicide by the hundreds at the gates of Baghdad," that U.S. troops were being "butchered" at the airport and that there were no "American infidels" in the city, when U.S. units could be seen just a short distance away.

With Marine and infantry units closing in on the city, Brig. Gen. Vincent Brooks, a U.S. military spokesman,

declared: "The dagger is clearly pointed at the heart of the Baghdad regime."

U.S. generals had earlier given the impression that they were in no hurry to move into Baghdad, even though they controlled the main access routes, suggesting instead that they would take their time to pacify the city. What happened was very different and typical of the boldness and deception of Gen. Tommy Franks' battle plan. In a show of force, U.S. armored units punched into central Baghdad on a "thunder run" designed to show that they could enter the city at will.

U.S. television networks showed footage of American soldiers relaxing on chairs inside one of Saddam's palaces, which they had seized. One soldier said he was about to take a shower in an opulent bathroom. It was a powerful military and psychological blow.

In Baghdad, the human cost of the war was becoming apparent. Red Cross officials reported "terrible" conditions in one of the city's hospitals. Doctors struggled to cope with a constant stream of civilian dead and injured, saying they were running short of anesthetics and other medical supplies.

To the south, British paratroopers walked unopposed into Basra, ending a lengthy standoff with determined local fighters.

U.S. forces meanwhile forced their way through central Baghdad, widening control of the city and pounding holdout Iraqi defenders, who offered fierce but sporadic resistance.

Marines in a battle for control of a bridge on the southeastern outskirts of Baghdad, April 6, 2003.

REUTERS/Oleg Popov

Marines search an urban area in an operation to take over the Rashid air base in Baghdad, April 8, 2003.

REUTERS/Oleg Popov

Iraqi men flash victory signs on the top of an anti-aircraft gun in the southern outskirts of Baghdad, April 6, 2003.

REUTERS/Goran Tomasevic

An Iraqi soldier waves a grenade launcher in front of a destroyed U.S. tank in Baghdad, April 6, 2003.

REUTERS/Goran Tomasevic

destroyed Iraqi Airways lane lies on the runway of aghdad airport surrounded y U.S. Army vehicles, April 6, 003. Taking the international rport two days earlier was n important strategic step nd sent a powerful message o the Iraqi leadership that .S. forces were on their oorstep.

EUTERS/Kai Pfaffenbach

An Iraqi civilian waves a makeshift white flag as he flees fighting in Basra, April 6, 2003.

REUTERS/Yannis Behrakis

A British army officer stands with her handgun at the ready as Iraqi civilians flee fighting in Basra, April 6, 2003.

REUTERS/Yannis Behrakis

An Iraqi soldier rides a motorcycle past a destroyed U.S. tank in Baghdad, April 6, 2003.

REUTERS/Goran Tomasevic

A U.S. Army Abrams tank with "Baghdad's nightmare" written on its cannon passes infantry troops near the Euphrates River as hundreds of armored vehicles push toward the outskirts of Baghdad, April 6, 2003.

REUTERS/Kai Pfaffenbach

Civilians raise their hands in surrender to British troops in front of a burning compound in a Basra neighborhood, April 6, 2003.

REUTERS/Yannis Behrakis

An image from Iraqi television shows what it says is Saddam Hussein visiting a residential area of the Iraqi capital, April 4, 2003. On that day, U.S. forces won a battle for control of Baghdad airport.

REUTERS/Iraqi Satellite Television/Handout

Iraqi Information Minister Mohammed Saeed al-Sahaf during a news conference in Baghdad, April 5, 2003. On this day, U.S. forces staged a raid into Baghdad for the first time and took the headquarters of a division of the Republican Guard.

REUTERS/Goran Tomasevic

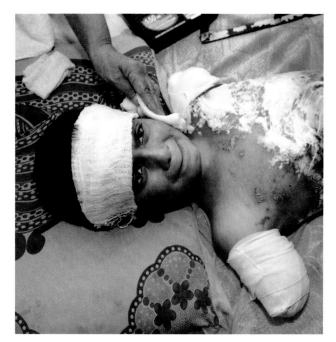

Ali Ismaeel Abbas, 12, wounded during an air strike, lies in a hospital bed in Baghdad, April 6, 2003. A missile left him badly maimed and orphaned, an icon of civilian suffering in the Iraq conflict. His father, pregnant mother, brother, aunt, three cousins and three other relatives who were at home with him were killed. U.S. forces flew Ali to Kuwait where surgeons vowed to fit him with the most sophisticated replacement limbs available. His case was highlighted in newspapers and on television screens around the world, sparking a flood of fund-raising appeals for Iraqi war victims.

REUTERS/Faleh Kheiber

Ali is examined by Kuwaiti plast surgeon Imad al-Najada (left) up arrival at Kuwait's Ibn Sina Hospi Burn Center, April 16, 2003. Al uncle and a nurse tend to him.

REUTERS/Stephanie McGehee

Ali is kissed by a Sheikh while lying in a hospital bed in the Baghdad suburb of Saddam City, April 15, 2003.

REUTERS/Chris Helgren

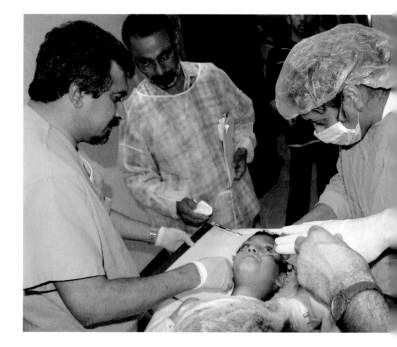

Kurdish "peshmerga" fighters watch an air strike on Iraqi government positions on the front line in territory newly taken by Kurds and U.S. forces after a retreat by Iraqi government forces from Kalak, west of Arbil, northern Iraq, April 3, 2003.

REUTERS/Caren Firouz

السيد صدام حسين رئيس مجلس قيادة الثورة رئيس جمهورية العراق
دار العربية للعلوم ــ بيدا

A U.S. Army combat engineer stands on a portrait of Saddam Hussein at Baghdad airport, April 7, 2003.

REUTERS/Kai Pfaffenbach

An Army captain removes a portrait of Saddam Hussein from a special VIP building near Baghdad airport, April 7, 2003. The U.S. military believes Saddam used this area of the airport.

REUTERS/Kai Pfaffenbach

Members of the Iraqi Republican Guard, dressed in civilian clothes, sit behind barbed wire at an abandoned Iraqi military base under the control of Marines in the Baghdad suburbs, April 8, 2003.

REUTERS/Oleg Popov

U.S. FORCES STORM THE HEART OF BAGHDAD

U.S. forces burst into central Baghdad on April 7 and encircled the Iraqi capital. Three days earlier Baghdad airport had fallen and on April 5 U.S. troops punched into the city for the first time seizing the headquarters of a Republican Guard Division

Saddam Hussein's rule over Iraq crumbled on April 9 and in scenes reminiscent of the fall of the Berlin Wall, a huge statue of Saddam was toppled in the city's center

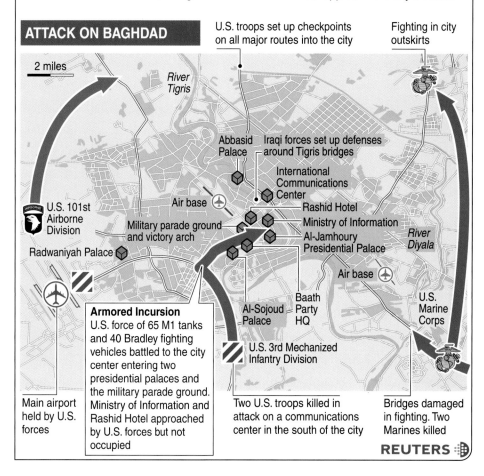

ATTACK ON BAGHDAD

U.S. troops set up checkpoints on all major routes into the city

Fighting in city outskirts

2 miles

River Tigris

Abbasid Palace

Iraqi forces set up defenses around Tigris bridges

International Communications Center

U.S. 101st Airborne Division

Air base

Rashid Hotel

Military parade ground and victory arch

Ministry of Information

Al-Jamhoury Presidential Palace

River Diyala

Radwaniyah Palace

Air base

Armored Incursion
U.S. force of 65 M1 tanks and 40 Bradley fighting vehicles battled to the city center entering two presidential palaces and the military parade ground. Ministry of Information and Rashid Hotel approached by U.S. forces but not occupied

Al-Sojoud Palace

Baath Party HQ

U.S. Marine Corps

U.S. 3rd Mechanized Infantry Division

Main airport held by U.S. forces

Two U.S. troops killed in attack on a communications center in the south of the city

Bridges damaged in fighting. Two Marines killed

REUTERS

Explosions caused by a U.S. air strike
on the Iraqi Planning Ministry building
in Baghdad, April 8, 2003.

REUTERS/Faleh Kheiber

The Tipping Point

Day 21

April 9

In a war fought under closer media scrutiny than any other in history, it was fitting that the collapse of Saddam Hussein's 24-year rule of Iraq came on live television.

Youths fixed a rope round the neck of a giant statue of Saddam in central Baghdad, and U.S. Marines hauled it over with an armored vehicle in front of crowds of cheering Iraqis, who dragged its severed head through the streets. In one of the strongest insults of the Arab world, men and boys beat Saddam's cast metal features with their shoes. The sight of Iraqis hacking at the statue's marble plinth with a sledgehammer recalled the fall of the Berlin Wall in 1989.

Before the statue came down, its head was briefly draped with the Stars and Stripes. However, Marines took that down and quickly replaced it with an Iraqi flag in a gesture to already inflamed sensibilities in the Arab world.

Endlessly repeated on U.S. television, the statue's collapse was greeted with satisfaction in Washington and London. "They got it down" was President Bush's reaction, while his close ally, British Prime Minister Tony Blair, was said to be "delighted." Defense Secretary Donald Rumsfeld said Saddam would take his place in the ranks of "failed dictators," such as Hitler, Stalin, Lenin and Ceausescu.

Exactly where Saddam and his immediate entourage were when the statue fell remained a mystery. Baghdad residents, however, felt ready to greet U.S. soldiers and also took the opportunity to loot the city. For ordinary Iraqis, it was perhaps as much a gesture of revenge against a brutal government as it was a means of enriching themselves. Everything that was not nailed down, from air conditioning units to giant urns, was removed by gangs of looters staggering under the weight of their spoils. Even the headquarters of the feared secret police was being looted when the Marines arrived.

Iraqis threw flowers and cheered as U.S. soldiers took control of their city. "No more Saddam Hussein," they cried. "We love you, we love you."

By that point, the Americans had fewer than 100 dead, and the British had fewer than 30. What Iraqi resistance they met during their three-week advance through the country was generally not hard to overcome, given their enormous advantage in firepower. Rather than stand and fight against Abrams and Challenger tanks, Iraqi forces had largely melted away, leaving their heavy weapons and ammunition behind them unused.

With Baghdad and the south under U.S. and British control, the northern cities of Mosul and Kirkuk were quick to fall, while Saddam's hometown, Tikrit, followed a few days later.

There was as yet no definitive evidence that any stocks of chemical or biological weapons had been found.

The campaign to topple Saddam had not been as easy as some U.S. hawks had suggested before the war, but, for its speed and aggression, it will probably go down in history as one of the most accomplished examples of armored maneuver warfare ever seen.

On May 1, Bush addressed the American people again, this time from the deck of the aircraft carrier USS Abraham Lincoln as it steamed toward the California coast and home.

"Major combat operations in Iraq have ended," the president said. "In the battle of Iraq, the United States and our allies have prevailed. And now our coalition is engaged in securing and reconstructing that country."

A mural of Saddam Hussein splattered with crude oil in Basra, April 9, 2003.

REUTERS/Yannis Behrakis

A Marine shows a portrait of Saddam Hussein that he tore down in a battle for control of a bridge on the southeastern outskirts of Baghdad, April 6, 2003.

REUTERS/Oleg Popov

U.S. forces search the Sheraton Hotel in Baghdad, April 9, 2003.

REUTERS/Goran Tomasevic

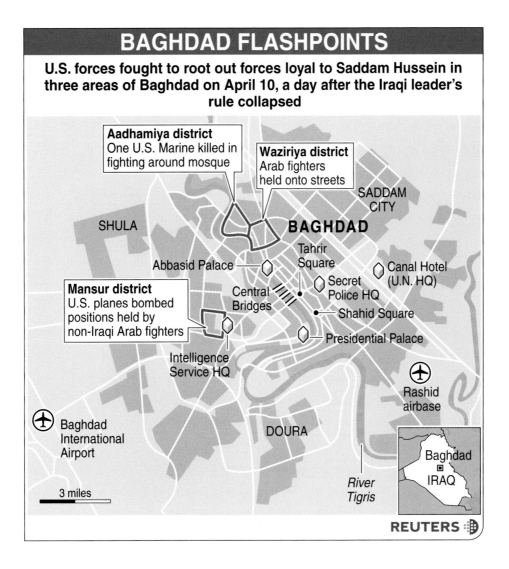

BAGHDAD FLASHPOINTS

U.S. forces fought to root out forces loyal to Saddam Hussein in three areas of Baghdad on April 10, a day after the Iraqi leader's rule collapsed

Aadhamiya district
One U.S. Marine killed in fighting around mosque

Waziriya district
Arab fighters held onto streets

SADDAM CITY

SHULA

BAGHDAD

Abbasid Palace

Tahrir Square

Canal Hotel (U.N. HQ)

Secret Police HQ

Mansur district
U.S. planes bombed positions held by non-Iraqi Arab fighters

Central Bridges

Shahid Square

Intelligence Service HQ

Presidential Palace

Rashid airbase

Baghdad International Airport

DOURA

Baghdad
IRAQ

River Tigris

3 miles

REUTERS

A U.S. soldier watches as a statue of Saddam Hussein falls in central Baghdad, April 9, 2003. In scenes reminiscent of the fall of the Berlin Wall in 1989, youths attacked the statue's marble plinth and looped a rope around its neck. A U.S. armored vehicle helped to topple it.

REUTERS/Goran Tomasevic

Iraqi soldiers march in the courtyard of the Martyrs' Monument in Baghdad, February 16, 2003.

REUTERS/Suhaib Salem

Just under two months later, Marines walk in front of the Martyrs' Monument, one of the landmarks of the Iraqi capital, during an operation to secure the center of Baghdad, April 9, 2003.

REUTERS/Oleg Popov

Kurdish "peshmerga" fighters hold the Kurdistan Democratic Party's yellow flag on a destroyed building at the top of Jabal Maqlub, a strategic mountain and military base east of Mosul, April 9, 2003. U.S. and Kurdish forces took Iraq's third largest city of Mosul two days later without a fight, sealing their victory in the north.

REUTERS/Caren Firouz

A Jordanian in Amman buries his head in his hands in front of a television showing a Marine draping the Stars and Stripes over the face of a statue of Saddam Hussein in Baghdad, April 9, 2003.

REUTERS/Ali Jarekji

Iraqi looters wave to a passing convoy of Marines as they push stolen generators in the suburbs of Baghdad, April 7, 2003.

REUTERS/Oleg Popov

n Iraqi man amid goods looted from government building in Baghdad, oril 9, 2003. Everything that was not ailed down, from air conditioning nits to giant urns, was removed by angs of looters staggering under e weight of their spoils.

UTERS/Goran Tomasevic

Kurdish women fighters celebrate entering the northern Iraqi oil town of Kirkuk, April 10, 2003.

REUTERS/Nikola Solic

Residents of Kirkuk wave the Kurdish flag on top of a pedestal where a statue of Saddam Hussein used to stand as they celebrate the ousting of Iraqi government forces, April 10, 2003.

REUTERS/Caren Firouz

An Army lieutenant walks inside one of Saddam Hussein's Baghdad palaces, April 13, 2003.

REUTERS/Goran Tomasevic

A bomb-damaged reception hall in one of Saddam Hussein's palaces in Baghdad, April 13, 2003.

REUTERS/Goran Tomasevic

An Army lieutenant looks at a mural in one of the Iraqi leader's Baghdad palaces, April 13, 2003.

REUTERS/Goran Tomasevic

Spc. Joseph Hudson

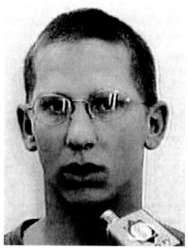

Pfc. Patrick Miller

Spc. Shoshana Johnson

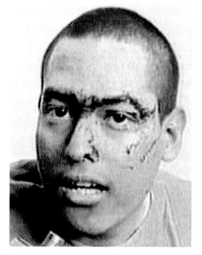

Spc. Edgar Hernandez

Sgt. James Riley

CWO David Williams

CWO Ronald D. Young Jr.

Combination picture compiled from video footage shown on Iraqi television of U.S. prisoners of war. The prisoners were rescued by Marines, who were conducting a house-to-house raid in the city of Samarra on April 13, 2003.

REUTERS/Iraqi TV

Seven U.S. prisoners of war rescued in Iraq by Marines emerge from an aircraft for hospital treatment in Kuwait, April 13, 2003.

A U.S. Defense Department image showing a deck of cards distributed to forces with each card separately identifying 55 Iraqi leaders whom the United States wants pursued, killed or captured, April 11, 2003. The cards were also distributed around Iraq in the form of posters and handbills.

REUTERS/Defense Department handout

Marines occupy Saddam Hussein's presidential palace in Tikrit, April 14, 2003. Tikrit, close to Saddam's birthplace, was considered his power base.

REUTERS/Chris Helgren

Iraq conflict timeline

■March 20
President Bush announces start of the campaign to oust President Saddam Hussein, saying selected targets were hit by air raids in an attempt to decapitate the Iraqi leadership.

Saddam appears on TV, three hours after the raids began, urging Iraqis to defend their country. It was impossible to determine when the broadcast had been recorded.

Iraq fires missiles at Kuwait, sending U.S. troops scrambling into chemical protective suits and setting air raid sirens blaring in Kuwait City.

■March 21
Invasion forces sweep into southern Iraq. Marines attack the port of Umm Qasr. British troops capture Faw peninsula and take control of oil installations.

Eight British soldiers and four U.S. airmen are killed in a helicopter crash on the Iraqi border.

U.S.-led forces unleash a devastating blitz on Baghdad. Missiles slam into Saddam s palaces and key government buildings.

The United States suffers first combat casualty.

■March 22
Seven killed, six Britons and one American, when two Royal Navy Sea King helicopters collide.

■March 23
A Royal Air Force Tornado jet is shot down by a U.S. Patriot missile near the Kuwait border in the first known friendly fire incident of the war.

Two U.S. soldiers are killed and 14 wounded in a grenade attack at a tented command center in Kuwait. A U.S. serviceman was arrested.

■April 2
U.S. troops attack Fedayeen fighters loyal to Saddam in Najaf, drawing fire from fighters hiding in one of the world s holiest Muslim shrines. U.S. commanders said they did not fire back on the Ali Mosque.

U.S. forces encircle Kerbala.

U.S. Brig. Gen. Vincent Brooks says U.S. troops have destroyed one of the six divisions of the Republican Guard defending Baghdad.

■April 3
Power goes off in most of Baghdad for the first time since the war began.

■April 4
U.S. forces seize control of Baghdad s Saddam International airport and rename it Baghdad International.

Iraqi television shows footage of what it says is Saddam visiting residential areas of Baghdad.

■April 5
U.S. forces enter Baghdad for the first time and take the headquarters of the Medina division of Saddam s Republican Guard.

■April 7
U.S. forces storm Baghdad, seizing two of Saddam s palace complexes.

U.S. aircraft drop four 2,000-pound bombs on a building after U.S. intelligence reports say Saddam and his sons Uday and Qusay might have been inside.

British paratroopers walk unopposed into the center of Iraq s second city, Basra, where residents warmly welcome them.

■April 8
A U.S. tank fires a shell at Palestine hotel in Baghdad packed with foreign journalists, killing a cameraman from Reuters and another from Spain s Tele 5, just hours after al-Jazeera says one of its correspondents was killed by American fire.

■ **March 24**
Britain confirms its first combat casualty, a soldier killed near Zubayr in southern Iraq.

■ **March 25**
Umm Qasr, where U.S. led forces have been trying for days to put down Iraqi resistance so that aid can be shipped in, is declared "safe and open."

A big convoy of Marines crosses the Euphrates River and Saddam Canal at Nassiriya, resuming their advance to Baghdad.

■ **March 26**
At least 15 people die in explosion in residential and commercial street in Baghdad's Shaab district. U.S. officials say the blast could have been caused by an errant missile or anti-aircraft artillery or missiles fired by the Iraqi military.

About 1,000 U.S. troops parachute into Kurdish-held northern Iraq and take control of an airfield.

■ **March 28**
A B-2 bomber drops two "bunker-buster" bombs on a downtown Baghdad communications tower.

At least 62 people are killed in an air strike that hit a Baghdad market.

■ **March 29**
A car bomb explodes at a U.S. checkpoint near the city of Najaf, about 100 miles south of Baghdad, killing four U.S. soldiers.

■ **March 31**
Marines enter the town of Shatra, 20 miles north of Nassiriya.

■ **April 2**
Marines seize a bridge over the Tigris River in central Iraq and take control of the main highway from Kut to Baghdad

■ **April 9**
Saddam's rule collapses as U.S. forces sweep into the heart of Baghdad, taking control of the capital and toppling a huge statue of the man who towered over the country for 24 years.

In New York, Iraq's U.N. ambassador, Mohammed Aldouri, says "the game is over" and he hopes the Iraqi people will soon be able to live in peace.

■ **April 10**
Kurdish fighters take the northern oil city of Kirkuk as U.S. troops mop up die-hard Saddam supporters in Baghdad.

Senior Iraqi Shi'ite leader Abdul Majid al-Khoei is killed by a mob at a mosque in the holy city of Najaf.

U.S. gains control of Qaim on key road to Syria, and captures more than 100 tanks north of Kerbala.

■ **April 11**
U.S. and Kurdish forces take Iraq's third city of Mosul without a fight, sealing their victory in the north.

U.S. military issues deck of cards depicting the 55 most-wanted Iraqi leaders. Almost two weeks later former deputy prime minister Tareq Aziz, the best-known public face of the old regime, surrenders to U.S. custody. He was among a growing number of senior figures being held. "They're collapsing like a house of cards," a Pentagon spokesman said.

■ **April 12**
Amid widespread looting in Baghdad, thieves make off with priceless antiquities from the National Museum.

■ **April 14**
Marines enter the center of Tikrit, Saddam's hometown, taking control of the Iraqi strongman's power base.

Photographers

Peter Andrews joined Reuters in 1991 during the first coup in Moscow. In 1996 he moved to Johannesburg and in 1999 became Chief Photographer for Eastern and Southern Africa and Nairobi. Andrews was embedded with U.S. forces in southern Iraq.

Tim Aubry is based in Washington D.C. He began his career with Reuters in 1988 and has a degree in photojournalism from Bowling Green University in Ohio. He was based in Doha, Qatar, during the conflict.

Yannis Behrakis was born in Athens in 1960 and has worked for Reuters since 1987. He has covered wars in the former Yugoslavia and in Chechnya as well as stories in Asia, Africa, the Middle East and Eastern Europe. He has won numerous awards for his work. Throughout the Iraq war, he was based in southern Iraq.

Fabrizio Bensch was born in 1969 in Berlin. He studied political science and has covered assignments all over Europe. He has been based in Berlin since 1992.

Jim Bourg has been Reuters Boston photographer since 1988, covering New England and traveling extensively throughout the United States and overseas.

Russell Boyce joined Reuters as a staff photographer in 1988 and has traveled the world extensively covering both news and sports stories. Boyce was embedded with the Royal Air Force in northern Iraq.

Desmond Boylan was born in 1964 in London. He worked for the Associated Press for three years before joining Reuters. Based in Madrid for six years, he was embedded with U.S. Marines and British Royal Marine commandos.

Kieran Doherty has worked for Reuters for his entire career. He is a staff photographer and is based in London. Doherty has won many awards, including the English Sports Council award for Image of the Year and Best Sports Photo in 1998.

Caren Firouz is an Iran-based photographer and covered the conflict from bases in Arbil, northern Iraq.

Paul Hanna was born in the United States in 1965 and moved to Madrid in 1987, where he started working with Reuters. He has since worked in London and Rome and has now moved back to Spain. In the Iraq conflict, he was aboard the USS Kitty Hawk.

Chris Helgren was based in Zagreb from 1992-96, throughout the Bosnian War. After that he had a wide variety of assignments. In October 2002, Helgren moved to the Gulf to organize photographic coverage of the expected war with Iraq. Starting from Kuwait, and traveling in an armored Land Rover, he was the first photographer into the southern city of Basra, made it into Baghdad and later arrived in the northern stronghold of Tikrit the day it fell to U.S. Marines.

Stephen Hird is a London-based photographer for Reuters and was embedded with British Royal Marine commandos.

Ali Jarekji is a 49-year old Syrian, who started working with Reuters in 1985. He covered the Lebanon war and since 1992, has worked from Jordan in many locations throughout the Middle East.

Vincent Kessler is a stringer with Reuters who is based in France.

Faleh Kheiber is Reuters chief photographer in Iraq. During the Iraq conflict, Faleh was based in Baghdad.

Kevin Lamarque has been with Reuters for 15 years, based in Hong Kong, London and the United States. Lamarque has covered major international news events as diverse as the troubles in Northern Ireland and the funeral of Princess Diana.

Jerry Lampen was born in Rotterdam in 1961 and became a news and sports reporter in 1981. In 1985 he joined United Photos in Haarlem, returning in 1987 to Rotterdam, where he began working with Reuters. Lampen was based in southern Iraq during the conflict.

Dylan Martinez was born in Barcelona in 1969 and moved to Britain a year later. He began taking pictures for Reuters in 1991 and has worked in Asia, based in Vietnam. He is based in Rome as chief photographer.

Stephanie McGehee has worked for Reuters since 1992 as a photographer in Kuwait. She regularly conducts photography seminars in the Arab Gulf region. Stephanie was born in the United States and has lived in the Middle East for more than 25 years.

Kai Pfaffenbach began working with Reuters in 1996. He remains based in Frankfurt. Pfaffenbach was part of the Reuters team of photographers covering the attacks of September 11, 2001. He was embedded with U.S. forces during the Iraq conflict.

Oleg Popov has been a photographer for the Bulgarian Telegraph Agency and Bulgarian Newspapers and Magazines. He began working for Reuters in 1990 and he has covered wars in the Balkans and Chechnya, as well as Iraq. During this latest conflict he was embedded with U.S. Marines.

Jason Reed was born in Sydney in 1970 and joined Reuters during his first year of college. He is based in Hong Kong and has worked extensively throughout Asia, as well as in Afghanistan and Pakistan. He was embedded with U.S. troops in Kuwait.

Damir Sagolj was born in Sarajevo in 1971 and worked with the Paris-based Sipa press agency for several years before joining Reuters as a photographer based in Bosnia. Sagolj was embedded with U.S. Marines.

Suhaib Salem studied journalism and media before joining Reuters as a photojournalist in 1997. He won a prize in the 2000 World Press Photography competition. Salem was located in Baghdad and then Gaza during the conflict.

John Schults was embedded aboard the USS Abraham Lincoln, USS Mobile Bay and USS Comfort during the Iraq conflict. He is based in Reuters Paris Bureau.

Nikola Solic was based in northern Iraq during the conflict.

Darren Staples is a freelance photographer, based in London.

Goran Tomasevic started working for Reuters as a freelance photographer in 1996 and cites covering the conflict in Kosovo as one of his greatest professional challenges. During the Iraq conflict, Tomasevic was with the Reuters team in Baghdad.

Darren Whiteside is a Reuters photographer who is normally based in Indonesia.

Contributors

Lance Bell was a founding member of Reuters News Graphics, which was set up in 1990.

Ricardo Carrera joined Reuters in 1995 and leads the graphics service's Spanish desk in Miami.

Ninian Carter, a graduate of Heriott-Watt University, Edinburgh, began his career in graphic design in 1991 at *The Edinburgh Evening News*. He later worked on *The Scotsman* and *The Observer* as well as with the JSI (news graphics) Agency in Paris. He has been with Reuters for five years.

David Cutler is senior researcher at Reuters Editorial Reference Unit in London. Born in Glasgow, Cutler started his career at London's Imperial War Museum. He later joined the BBC and then, in 1987, Reuters. Cutler now leads the unit that provides research and information for Reuters journalists around the world.

Giles Elgood has been a correspondent for Reuters for more than 20 years, reporting from more than 30 countries on five continents. He has worked as a defense specialist in London, covering the first Gulf War. He was assigned to the Balkans during the hostilities in Bosnia and to NATO headquarters in Brussels for the Kosovo conflict. He is based in Washington, D.C.

Jim Peet joined Reuters in 1995 from the British Press Association's graphics desk.

Jason Pickersgill qualified in Newspaper Design and Information Graphics at Newcastle College and has worked with Reuters as a freelancer since 2001. He has worked for Britain's *Independent* and *Observer* newspapers, as well as the BBC.

Paul Scruton became a full-time Reuters graphic journalist in 1998 after freelancing for the service since 1996.

Mike Tyler, a freelancer for Reuters News Graphics in London since 1997, studied graphic design at John Moores University, Liverpool, and worked on a range of corporate identity projects before establishing Mapstyle, a custom map design service, in 1994.

About Reuters

Reuters (www.about.reuters.com), the global information company, provides indispensable information tailored for professionals in the financial services, media and corporate markets. Our information is trusted and drives decision making across the globe based on our reputation for speed, accuracy and independence. We have 16,000 staff in 94 countries, including some 2,400 editorial staff in 197 bureaux serving approximately 130 countries, making Reuters the world's largest international multimedia news agency.